Unleashing
The Power To

Write Your Own

Life Story

A step-by-step Handbook For

First Time Writers

By
Richard McInnis

ISBN 978 - 1514846582
Copyright © July 1, 2015 by Richard McInnis
6839 Wellington Drive
Dexter, MI 48130

The Content and purpose
Of This Step By Step Handbook

First, The Content

of this Handbook includes much of the information
on the author's site, lifestory-stepbystep.com,
organized here in a handy, portable, book-style
format for quick and easy reference,
wherever you are

Plus

This Handbook includes
information not found on the site,
in the form of examples, exhibits, note pages and
ideas from the author's own Life Story,

The Ornery Rooster
And Other Humorous Encounters
My Story So Far

And Then The Purpose
(Continued Next Page)

The purpose
of this Life Story Writing Handbook is

To present the step-by-step life story writing process in a practical, portable handbook that will have you writing in minutes, wherever you are.

To provide solid, proven techniques such as *focused-writing* and *one-little-story-at-a-time* to help you start building your life story today.

To provide spaces for notes, designed to get you involved and off to a fast start by putting ideas to work on-the-spot!

To provide a collection of exhibits and examples from the author's own life story, to demonstrate how to prepare selected front and end support documents.

To help you *unleash your power to write*, by identifying and dumping common wrong ideas that keep people from writing.

To present a quick, down-to-earth, organized way to get started writing your Life Story today,

To outline the steps in the writing process, so you'll always know where you are and what's next.

To provide information that will help you set your own writing goals, ranging from a few stories collected in a loose-leaf binder to a hard-cover book.

For All

Who have an interesting story to

share, and who are seeking an

easy, step by step way to transform

their memories and experiences into a

tangible form to be enjoyed

by family and others

for years to come,

(continued next page)

May You discover

through the step by step process

described in this Handbook,

How To

Unleash The Power

To Write and Share Your Story,

by

ditching ideas that block our efforts

in exchange for

a fresh start.

Table Of Contents

The Content and Purpose
Of This Step By Step Handbook

Dedication
For All Who Seek An Easy Step By Step Way
To write Their Life Story

Introduction
The Step By Step
Life Story Writing Handbook

My name is Richard and as a gift to my family, I recently finished writing my story,

The Ornery Rooster
And Other Humorous Encounters,
My Story So Far

After sharing it with a friend, she said, "I'd love to write about my journey like that, but the thought of it seems so overwhelming. I don't have the slightest idea of how to begin!"

Unfortunately, this is the feeling of most first-time writers. But I have good news for you. Writing your personal story does not have to be overwhelming, if you break it down in to manageable steps. And, I'll show you how, step-by-step.

- How to start writing today - and how to keep writing day-after-day.

- Where to start (not on chapter one!) and build your life story piece by piece.

- How to unleash your power to write, by ditching the blocks, those scoundrels that stop first-time writers in their tracks.

- How to move from feeling overwhelmed to the feeling of joy in the journey through a project you'll love.

These down-to-earth ideas and simple steps that I'll show you came from the hard-earned experience of writing my own story.

As a career teacher, I always loved helping others find simpler, easier and more practical ways of doing things. And that's what I am doing in this *Handbook,* showing you more efficient and effective ways of reaching writing goals of your choice.

Goals Of Your Choice?

Yes, you get to choose your own goals! And this *Handbook* will help you do that in chapter 7. Whatever your life writing goals, the entire process is here to guide you, step-by-step.

- If you just want to write and collect a few favorite stories from your life experiences, or

- If you want to go all the way by writing and printing a book, telling your story so far, or

- If you want to end up somewhere between writing a few stories or a complete book.

Use the space below to identify your writing goals as you see them now, before using this Handbook:

_____

_____

_____

_____

_____

_____

_____

Suggestions
For Using This Handbook

This Handbook consists of 10 Chapters, which you are encouraged to explore first in any order, according to your interest. Then check out the specific areas where you might find help below:

Already started to write your story? Jump in at a place where you have questions or have encountered problems.

Stumped or having trouble getting started? Check out the information on *Unleashing Your Power To Write - Booting Writer's Block,* to discover and dump ideas that might be holding you back.

Need a little motivational boost? Check out the information on *Why Write Your Life Story,* You just might unleash the power of a strong motive. The reasons might light your fire sufficient to inspire and motivate you to achieve your desired goal.

--or--

Ready for a fresh start right now?

-- My Suggestion --

Jump right into
The Handbook Chapter One,
for an overview of the Step By Step Writing Process,
and then move around to the other chapters
according to your interests.

Chapter 1
Let's Write A Little Story

"Write a little story?

"Who . . . me?"

Yes, you. You've been thinking about it for awhile now, and finally the day comes. Let's imagine, you're having a warm experience while socializing with a group of friends, that sort of floats you over the top.

Listen in . . .

You and your friends are enjoying life, laughing and having a ball, telling one story after another.

You tell a true, knee-slapping story, something funny you experienced years ago.

You are engaged, laughing, excited, on-fire with enthusiasm as you talk.

Your friends are engaged, listening and bursting with laughter as they share this joyful moment.

You decide that this would be a good little story to include in your overall life story. You can't wait to get home and *write* your little story.

You've made your decision. You are ready to write!

-- Now --
Recall one of those stories
that you've told so
many times before

and then

take 15 minutes

to write that little story
that you just love to tell over and over,
and that someday you would love
to include in your overall
Life Story

Be sure to time yourself, and stop at the end of 15
minutes even if your story is not yet complete.

Take 15 Minutes To Write Now
And at the end of the 15 minutes come back and
continue reading

How did you do, writing that little 15 minute story?
Were you able to write with ease during this time,
without stopping, and with no problem deciding
what to write?

Were you able to finish a rough draft of your story
within the 15 minute time limit?

Did you use the entire 15 minutes, or did you quit
writing before your time was up, not knowing what
else to include in your story?

If you were able to fill the timed 15 minute period to fluently write your little story without stopping, then you are well on your way to writing your life story,

because that is the very basis of the Step By Step Life Story Writing Process! Good for you! Put a smiley face by this paragraph!

However, you still might choose to sharpen your skills even more by increasing your awareness of the 5 common blocks that cause problems for many writers.

Unfortunately, many people find themselves staring at a blank page during this assignment, not knowing how or where to start writing.

If you were *NOT* able to write a rough draft of this little story, *fluently without stopping*, indicating that something was holding you back, or

If you were *NOT* able to complete a rough draft of your little story within the time limit, indicating that you might have been spending time on trying to *create* a story, *editing as you wrote,* or *focusing on other mechanics of writing* that might have affected the free flow of your thoughts, or

If you were *NOT* able to recall enough about your story to write for most of the 15 minutes, indicating that you might be focused on your most immediate thoughts vs. focused on a specific memory,

Then, chances are you were stumped by "*it*", more commonly known as some form of Writer's Block, and before going on, you should take time to check out the following common *wrong ideas* that strangle our writing efforts and stump us dead-in-our-tracks when we try to write our story.

Here are five big trouble makers, and you might even discover others. Check out each one to see how their deceptive misunderstandings have the power to hold you back.

- The idea that you have to create-your-story
- The idea that linear-writing-is the only way to accomplish your writing goal
- The idea that you must edit as you write
- The idea that a bound-book is the only worthy goal
- The idea that you can put your life story on some other media without initially writing it

You can unleash your power to write by becoming aware of and dumping these wrong ideas that might be holding you back.

Next - Go to the section of this Handbook on Writer's Blocks, and check out any that might be standing in your way, and then return to this page to continue reading a full description of The Step By Step Process of Life Story Writing.

The Step By Step
Life Story Writing Process

Life Story writing is easy, when we approach it Step
By Step, One little story at a time.

Writing a life story Step by Step involves, starting with a fresh mindset, by

- Ditching false ideas that strangle our power to write before we ever pick up our pen.
- Finding a motivating reason to write, and
- Getting to 'know thyself' - choosing *our* best time, best place and best methods to write.
- Choosing A topic to write about, from our own list of little stories that we want to be sure to include, and from the use of a variety of other writing prompts and ideas for little stories that might fit in our overall Life Story, but with no immediate concern about *where* they might fit in.
- Using *focused-writing*, a writing process that allows us to open the floodgates and write without filtering, whatever our conscious and subconscious memories pour out, by writing as fast as we can.
- Collecting a rough draft of each little story, and placing the rough draft copy in any order, in a binder prepared for this purpose.

Once we open the gates with our *fresh mindset,* we can easily slip into the *writing cycle groove,* and we easily

Choose a topic,
Write using the focused-writing technique
Collect
Repeat

And we continue this *writing-cycle*
many times before going on.

by

Choosing another topic
Writing using the focused writing technique,
Collecting - Repeating
over and over,
until we have collected
many, many, many little stories.

And That Is How
We Write The Story Of Our Life

Step by Step
One Story At A Time

We will decide later where each little story fits in
if it does
and then edit
and make changes
and corrections and adjustments
and perhaps even tweak and re-write

L-A-T-E-R   B-U-T   N-O-T   N-O-W

Focused Writing
What Is It, And How Does It Work?
A Skill To Develop

Life Story writing is more easily accomplished when we are able to bypass certain left-brain characteristics such as the compulsion to continuously edit, check grammar and spelling and re-write before going on.

These are all actions that slow us down and take our focus off the *story* when writing. *Focused writing is a technique* that helps us to temporarily bypass these stumbling blocks and focus on the story.

Focused Writing involves
giving your full, undivided attention
to the s-t-o-r-y you are trying to write
by writing as fast as you can to help you bypass
the temptation to edit, correct grammar and spelling
and re-write before going on.

Focused writing takes practice, but you'll develop the skill quickly once you begin to feel the results!

It might be helpful to imagine that you are running to catch a flight and that you need to get your message (story) off to your friend before you leave.

Hurry! Your flight is boarding.
What do you want to tell your friend?
Focus - For now, it's only the *message* that counts!
Last call for boarding. Focus! Don't stop to edit.
Finish your story.
Don't miss your flight!

Why the rush when writing?

The 'rush' helps you to recall good stories from your conscious and subconscious memories without your left brain strangling them with the details of editing, making corrections and changes.

Writing fast forces you to focus on the story while you temporarily bypass the mechanics of writing.

While focus-writing, it might also help to pretend that you are "telling" your story to someone who is friendly and non-judgmental toward you or your writing.

Why pretend that you are orally telling your story? Because you're no doubt already *good at telling* stories. But when you try to *write* them you often encounter some kind of writer's block. So pretending that you're *telling* the story frees you from common hang-ups people often have about writing.

Why a friendly, non-judgmental listener? Because we so often cripple under unfriendly judgment, even in our imagination. On the other hand, friendly support gives us encouragement and confidence to focus on the big idea (*the story*) while temporarily overlooking the mechanical errors of writing.

The value of focused writing?
It helps to connect our mind directly to the story, while sliding past technical details.

The result is better stories and more enjoyment in writing. After focused-writing, you'll look back at the *story* (not the technical details) and say, "Wow! I can write neat stories!" *Technical details can and will be handled later.*

You can practice focused-writing anytime.   Try it. Just choose a topic you're interested in, (any topic, not just a life story topic) and begin writing about it. Write for 15 minutes nonstop. Keep in mind, during your initial writing, it's the *story* that's important, not the mechanics of writing.

Life Story writing can be a joy when you focus on the story. Focused writing might take a little practice, but once you get the hang of it, you'll love it, because *it makes writing seem so effortless.*

Remember, it might help to pretend that you are *"telling"* your story to someone. Therefore, write as if a person is in front of you listening, and tell (write) your story to the person *quickly without stopping.*

Go to the next page now, and follow all eight instructions for focused-writing, and then write some (little) Story that might become a part of your overall life story.

Focused-Writing Instructions

1. Find a quiet place where you will not be interrupted for 15 minutes.

2. Choose any *one* of the topics from the list of Life Story Topics To Write About (Chapter 5).

3. Write a little story (a page or two). Have no concern for where your story might fit in your overall Life Story. Decide that later.

4. Time yourself – write nonstop for 15 minutes.

5. *Write* as fast as you can. Review page 15, *What Is Focused-writing* before you start. Remember to imagine you're running to catch a flight, or some other thought of rushing.

6. Get the main ideas that you want to tell about this one topic down on paper. The story is more important than any other details. Shortcuts and abbreviations such as those used in phone texting are acceptable for now.

7. Don't stop writing. Unleash any blocks and write freely. Open the floodgates and let your subconscious pour out the words, writing whatever it tells you, in whatever order, without filters. You can straighten it out later.

8. When you finish place your story in a loose leaf binder with enough space to collect all of the stories you will be writing. Editing, corrections and changes come later - not now.

Be patient with yourself. You might have to practice focused-writing a few times before you get really good at it. But stick with it. The pay-off is well worth your efforts. And, of course, the more you write the better you'll get!

How Do You Write A Life Story?

Step-by-Step
one little story at a time!
Choose a topic - Focus Write - Collect - Repeat!
Choose a topic - Focus Write - Collect - Repeat!
And just keep writing.

The more you write these little stories, the better you'll get, the more fun you'll have writing, and the easier it'll become to recall stories to write about, as one little story jogs your memory for another little story to write.

And soon you'll have a binder full of these little stories that you can begin to sequence in some kind of theme to create your overall life story. More about that in another chapter.

Write stories about
things you've learned and the fun you've had,
what makes you tick and where you've been
what you've done and what's still on your bucket list
and maybe even some of your struggles.

Grab a sheet of paper and make notes of other topic ideas to add to your list, and then place your list at the front of your binder.

Does The Step by Step Process Work?

MY STORY - *An Example*

After deciding that I would like to write the Story Of My Life, I battled writer's block for more than 15 years! Whenever I sat down to *write,* I was overwhelmed and crippled by wrong ideas. With increased awareness, I began to analyze and dump ideas that were holding me back. I soon discovered that writing was more fun and easier.

Dumping what had been blocking my progress truly unleashed my power to write!

Once I stumbled on to this Step-by-Step, focused writing approach, I turned out a 212 page story of my life in three months, beginning-to-off-the-press, after stumbling for over 15 years!

I discovered that writing in itself is not that time consuming, once we

- ditch the false ideas that cause writer's block,
- know what to write,
- know how to get started,
- start using the Step-by-Step, one-story-at-a-time approach, opening the floodgates as one story leads to another.

And finally, I discovered that we not only come up with many great stand-alone stories from our list, but we also begin to see possible themes emerge for our overall Life Story.

2 - Unleashing Your Power To Write
-- Booting Writer's Block --

WRITER'S BLOCK is one of the greatest challenges in writing. It is very simply something that mentally blocks us (usually a wrong idea) from getting started or being productive in writing.

- It causes brain-freeze.
- It drowns our ideas and memories.
- It puts a lock on our ability to think.
- It causes us to sit and stare at a blank sheet of paper.
- It makes us feel stupid, and then we quit.

Writer's block is fueled by false ideas and misunderstandings that continue to cause us problems, unless we clear them up in the beginning. There's no half way. We must boot them out for good!

MY STORY
An Example Of Writer's Block

During my early frustrating efforts at writing, the teacher-in-me continued to search for what was holding me back. Why did I always end up staring at a blank sheet of paper when I sat down to write?

It was during this long process of can't-get-started-searching that I discovered the following five blocks that were stopping me in my tracks.

1 - The create-my-story-blocker

2 - The linear-writing-blocker

3 - The editing-blocker

4 - The bound-book-blocker

5 - The writing-unnecessary-blocker

After I got a clear understanding of how these blocks held me back, and how to avoid them, I was on my way to writing with ease.

I faced the monsters head-on and was able to write and accomplish more in less time.

But time isn't the only factor of importance. It might realistically take months or years to complete our life story, but by clarifying these misunderstandings that hold many writers back, my time became more productive when I did sit down to write.

My writing became less overwhelming and I found more joy in the writing process as I became more productive.

But be on guard. These characters are mischievous.

Even after you think you have booted them out, they have a way of sneaking back unnoticed, until one day you again find yourself staring at a blank sheet of paper, unable to write, only to realize that, "Oh, oh! Writer's Block again!"

Once you understand what's strangling your power to write, it only takes minutes to kick the culprit out again and get back on the road to productive writing.

The Create-My-Story Blocker

Writer's Block #1 operates under the false idea that we have to *create* our stories.

The truth is,
We don't have to create our life story. Our story already exists - we have already lived it.

Our job is to access our conscious and subconscious memories to *recall the story* so we can record it in some tangible form.

This blocker comes about as a result of the misunderstanding of the term *life writing*.

Life writing involves recalling our story and recording it in some tangible form. That might be on paper, on the computer, on an audio recorder or by some other means.

Yes, writing a life story involves recalling and recording. *Not creating.*

Fiction writers are faced with the task of *creating* characters, plots, stories and more. But most of us are not fiction writers. Most of us are not all that good at *creating* characters, plots and stories. It's easier than all that! We're writing a true story that has already been lived up to the current time.

We are not only the main character of our life story, but we are also the author, and we know the story better than anyone.

Yes, we have already experienced our Life Story up to the present moment. Therefore, we don't have to create it. We just have to recall it.

Our job is to merely capture those little stories that make up our overall life story, and get them down on paper in an interesting and meaningful manner.

To do this, we have to,

access our memories, and then

select and write about those successes, struggles, good and maybe even not-so-good experiences, that we want to include in our life story, to let people know who we are and how we got to where we are today.

This broader understanding of the meaning of *writing* as used in Life Story Writing, tosses Writer's Block #1 in the ditch for good, strangling leash and all! No more sitting, staring at blank sheets of paper trying to *create* stories. Just recall and write stories you already know.

Remember, each scoundrel blocker that you ditch *unleashes your power to write* and brings you a big step closer to writing your stories freely. This means you won't feel so stressed and frustrated, and you'll get more joy from writing your life story.

So, before you leave, be sure to check out the other Writer's Blocks. OK, you've booted this one. Now go on to another. You'll be amazed at how unleashed you'll feel with these cripplers out of your way!

The Linear-Order-Blocker

Writer's Block #2 operates under the false idea that writing is a linear process. This false idea stops us in our tracks. It leads us to believe that in writing our Life Story, we must First - decide on the title, then prepare a Table of Contents, and then write the chapters in order.

This false idea of *how* and *where* to start, stumped me for years. But when I finally discovered the most productive order of writing, I began to write with ease and enjoyment.

The First Truth Is,
We shouldn't even think about a title, table of contents or chapters until most of our writing is done. So, how and where do we start writing our life story?

First,
We learn to ignore the Writer's Block that says we should follow a certain order, and begin thinking about and making,

- a list of topics and ideas (in any order) that we think we would like to write about, and

- a list of the little stories waiting to be told that we already know we want to include.

Then,
We begin writing little stories, stories and more stories from our lists, *in any order,*

And Then
As we write these little stories, our memory kicks in and we discover that one story or idea leads to another. So we continue writing and collecting rough drafts of our stories, and adding new topics and ideas to our list, and writing -- and collecting -- and adding.

And for now, we just keep writing, more little stories, more little stories, and writing and collecting,

- Even though, we do not yet know,
- If the stories will fit in our overall Life Story,
- How the stories will fit, or
- Where the stories will fit

And, as we write,
Ideas for a theme begin to emerge. Then later on, after we've written many, many stories, we begin to sort them to fit the emerging theme. Some might fit

while others have to be tweaked, re-written or maybe even not used.

The Second Truth Is,
A title for our Life Story, the chapter titles and a table of contents all grow out of what we've been writing. *They do not dictate by telling us what to write. They are decided after writing many stories.*

Therefore, don't let this old false idea bully you, and keep you from getting started.

A title for your Life Story and a table of contents (if you decide to use one) are both developed after the bulk of your writing is completed.

The-Editing-Blocker

Writer's Block #3 operates under the false idea that we must edit and make corrections in wording, punctuation, spelling and grammar as we write.

This false idea is a monster that strangles a good story before completion of the first sentence. *Editing to make corrections as we write might result in a pretty sentence - but it might also strangle your story!*

The Truth Is,
Our initial writing should be *focused writing,* without filters and without stopping to edit or make corrections. We'll be back to do that later. This focused writing process, (non-editing-as-we-write) allows our conscious and subconscious to pour out the real story as we experienced it, feelings and all.

In our initial writing of a story, it is the story that is all important, not the wording, spelling, punctuation and grammar.

Our goal in the initial writing is to get the story down as it was experienced. We can go back later to rearrange details, make corrections in wording, spelling, punctuation and grammar.

Editing focuses on the mechanics of the writing process, not on accessing and recording memories. In fact, we as writers, may even choose to have someone else do our editing.

But accessing our memories, deciding what was and is of importance to us, deciding what to write about, these are tasks best left to us as writers of our Life Story.

The truth is,
We write about experiences, successes, failures, achievements, relationships, goals and more, all from our perspective.

And while many might be able to edit our work, making corrections in punctuation, spelling and grammar, no one can express the feelings from our perspective better than we can.

Editing comes after writing. It is not a part of our initial writing. So, *don't strangle a good story by trying to edit too early!* Know that changes and corrections will get their proper attention at the right time. But not during your first writing.

The Bound-Book Blocker

Writer's Block #4 mistakenly leads us to believe that the only worthy goal of writing is to end up with a bound book. The task of writing a bound book seems overwhelming to many, and scares writers from starting.

While striving to end up with a bound book might be a worthy goal for many writers, there are many worthy options for an end product other than a bound book. (See Goal Options info, pages 69-77).

This blocker keeps many from even starting to write their life story. The feeling is, "If I don't end up with a bound and printed book as a result of my writing, the stories that I've written are of no value and my efforts have been wasted."

The feeling that any writing you do, less than a complete bound book, can be overwhelming and stop you before you even get started. It causes us to accept a sort of *what's the use*" attitude. "I know I can't write a book, so why bother writing at all."

The truth is,
Writing and collecting stories or just making notes about our experiences in life is not a waste of time, no matter how you choose to preserve your efforts.

I have seen bits and pieces of Life Stories hidden in file boxes with financial papers. The families loved these treasures, and enjoyed reading them over and over.

I have talked with families who retrieved and treasured hand-written journals that amounted to Life Stories of their loved ones.

I recently attended a funeral where the value of little stories of life became even more apparent to me and to others mourning the loss, even though the stories were gathered from bits and pieces of information retrieved from the personal belongings of the deceased.

Story after story was told about the fun-loving personality, good times and loving relationships of the deceased.

References made to saved messages and clippings retrieved from her purse and refrigerator door documented how she touched so many lives.

For an hour, I observed family and friends cherish these little stories about their beloved, with a feeling of pride and comfort.

Yes, your stories are precious and valuable *in any form, not only in a book.* Even a simple collection of miscellaneous, handwritten stories and experiences is a family treasure to pass on.

But keep in mind, only YOU know the stories stored in your memory, so you must dig them out and get them on paper. You'll find that once you get digging, the process builds its own momentum.

Writing our Life Story is a step by step process. Each step is a worthy goal in itself. You may choose how many steps you want to complete, and *You always have the option to stop and rest.* Your memories are there for you to recall and write about, on *your* schedule.

The step-by-step process is designed to guide you as far as you want to go, whether that be an end product of a finished, printed bound book, or a mere written collection of stories and experiences. Your results will be cherished.

The Writing-Is-Unnecessary Blocker

Writer's block #5 operates under the false idea that actual "writing" is not necessary for digital, video or other higher tech ways of preserving our stories.

However, if we don't WRITE our stories, then under pressure, we risk the possibility of

- wasting costly studio time as we get help organizing our story for oral delivery.

- using costly studio time to re-do problem areas resulting from lack of written preparation.

- forgetting important story details, story punch lines, or even the best placement of whole stories.

- not sequencing our Life Story in a logical, interesting fashion,

- never getting started with our Life Story, because we need the step by step writing process itself to help us dig out and organize the story of our life.

Remember, only you know your stories, and only you can capture them, because only you are in charge of your memory bank. And you are the best one to refine and present them with genuine feeling, as you experienced them.

Can you do all this without at least an outline that
- includes all the stories you want to include?
- organizes the stories into an interesting sequence or theme?
- allows you to tell your stories in just the right place, with genuine feeling, emphasis and punch, just as you experienced them?

The writing process results in something concrete that we can get our hands on.

- It gives us a chance to see the whole picture.

- It also gives us the opportunity to make our work more interesting by allowing us to expand, contract, refine, tweak, enhance, slant and more.

Therefore, actual writing is very basic to all other ways of preserving our Life Story.

Also, the writing process does something very positive and personal for us. It gives us the opportunity to get in touch with and re-live experiences, and to re-evaluate, reframe and re-think them before sharing them.

The writing process in itself can be cathartic, as it helps us to gain a new perspective of our life.

Missing important information and parts of our stories is a risk if we don't have a written script, an outline or notes to work with, no matter what the electronic media.

Best suggestion?
Get your life story on paper first, even if only in long-hand. Then decide which media you would like to use to share your story with others.

With a written manuscript, you'll be ready for digital, video, online or any other type of recording, as well as ready for the printer.

In addition, you will have experienced the joy of re-living and clarifying certain aspects of your life during the writing process.

The step-by-step process is designed to help you prepare your written stories so you will be ready for whatever choice of media you choose to preserve and share your Life Story.

Also, be sure to read, *Do I need to write my story? chapter 7, goals and decisions, page 78.*

Identifying what stumps us when we sit down to write is the biggest step in overcoming a block.

Use the space below to identify any stumbling blocks you have encountered when you sat down to write, that might be holding you back.

_____

_____

_____

_____

_____

_____

_____

_____

_____

_____

_____

_____

3 - *Why Write A Life Story?*
The Power Of A Strong Motive

Why write your life story? This is a very important question to consider before beginning a life writing project. Why?

Because having a motivating reason, whatever it might be, provides the fuel you'll need to sustain your efforts and achieve your goal.

Here are some common and powerful reasons that might motivate you to write a Life Story:

- It is a precious and priceless gift of inspirational stories for loved ones, that can be passed down for generations to come.

- It provides the opportunity to share wisdom and valuable insights gained from lessons learned, in a non-preaching, story-like way.

- It has the potential to provide personal benefits for you the writer in the form of release from lingering issues and conflicts. Reflecting on the past during the writing process, provides the opportunity to sort out chosen experiences, and to clarify and reframe them from a more positive perspective.

Do any of the above reasons really stir your blood? Do any really give you the boost that makes you want to sit down and get started?

MY STORY - *An Example.* May I share a little story with you, about *MY* reasons for writing a story about my life? I pondered this question of WHY for years before I actually began to write.

- What should I write about?
- Who would even want to read my story?
- Of what value would it be, thinking that if the story wasn't good enough to publish and make me a millionaire it would be useless!

Still, I continued to have the urge to write. And the only thing I could think of writing about revolved around the happenings and events of my life. (Circle Thinking!)

As time passed, my growing children began saying, "Dad, you should write a book". Finally, one day I said, "I have no idea of how to write a book. What should I write about?"

Surprisingly, they had answers.

- "Write all the stories you tell us (over and over) about what life was like for you when you were growing up,"
- "Write about all the things you did as a child",
- "Write about things We did while we were growing up",
- "And be sure to include that funny story *you keep telling* over and over, about your Aunt Evelyn spilling the spaghetti in her lap at your dinner table when you were a kid, and the laughter that followed."

Not only did they have ideas about what I should write, but they also had ideas for stories about themselves that I could include.

As I watched our children grow, get their education and juggle families, careers and budgets to get ahead and maintain a comfortable life style, I began to realize that I had already experienced many of the normal challenges of life they were facing, and perhaps by example, I held the potential of a precious gift in the form of *Valuable Insights and Wisdom to Share. (But certainly, not titled this!)*

And finally, from my life-time experience of journal writing, I was aware of the joy as well as the *Personal Benefits for The Writer,* in reflecting on chosen experiences from the past.

This part of the Handbook discusses some typical and powerful reasons why people take time to write a story about their life.

Your Life Story
A Special Precious and Priceless Gift

As I considered my children's urgings to write, a life story, I began to see the importance to them from a new perspective. They weren't asking me to write a best seller or to write something that would make me a millionaire -- instead they wanted,

- stories about me and my life as I was growing up on our farm,

- stories (many of which they already knew) from my perspective about themselves and our family lives together as they were growing up,

- stories about my life after they grew up, married and left home,

- family stories they could read, re-read and enjoy as they re-lived the past, much like we would look through an old picture album, re-live and laugh about the changes in our lives and what life is like today compared to what it used to be like, and

- stories they could eventually pass on to their children.

Their urgings provided just enough energy to fan the flame of interest I already had in writing my Life Story, so I started writing.

But it wasn't until I completed the project a few months later that I *really* realized the importance to my children of my story.

In a Thank-You note, my daughter explained how much the book meant to her, and how the writing seemed to strengthen our family bonds.

She went on to say that even now with her own family, the stories reminded her of how important she is to our overall family, and that she would like to keep and pass down many of the family rituals that kept us bonded.

These comments from my daughter made me realize that a Life Story from a parent is not only,

- a very personal, precious and priceless gift *from* the one who lived the story, but also

- a very special gift *for* children and other family members, as well as

- a positive, warm reminder that (as the song goes), 'We Are Family".

So truthfully, I *started* my story, like my kids used to say, *"just because I wanted to!"* But once I finished it, I experienced an even greater satisfaction. I had truly given, a very *precious and priceless gift.*

Your Life Story
Valuable Insights and Wisdom To Share

While writing my Life Story, I came to realize that stories about various challenges I encountered on the road to success and how I responded, contained an abundance of non-preaching and often humorous lessons in interesting story form, that might be of potential value to others.

For example, I feel that my varied career journey has many lessons for younger family members starting out. My experiences ranged from farm helper to retail store clerk to filling station attendant to musician to accounting, to teacher to sales to corporate work and finally back to teaching, where I discovered the joy of right work.

Practical lessons can be found in these stories for any reader trying to sort out interests, abilities and values as they travel their own career journey.

I inherited a great work ethic from my parents that served me well, and the importance of that ethic shines at the root of my stories.

Another example of a story that carries a great message in a non-preaching way is my story about early financial struggles that strapped me until I learned better ways of handling money.

My decision to finally make a change and live on a cash basis within the limits of what I earned, and the positive results that followed, is an inspiring story that might be of help to many readers.

You too, have learned a lot during your life through your achievements and successes and yes, even through your set-backs.

And you have a lot of valuable wisdom and insights to share with readers now and in generations to come, through stories they might find encouraging, inspiring, motivating and otherwise of value to them.

When you start writing, using the techniques presented in this Handbook, you'll be amazed at how your stories will pour out from the storehouse of information you've accumulated, and how that will prove valuable to others.

- Stories of things you've learned the hard way.
- Insights and wisdom you have acquired through experience over the years.
- Inspiring stories of overcoming obstacles and hardships that readers would find encouraging and motivating in their own efforts to build a good life.

Yes, the experience of writing your Life Story is rich with heartwarming opportunities for you to share all you have learned through experience, in non-threatening story form.

Also, the *Personal Benefits for You The Writer* ranks high on the list of motivational reasons to write your story.

Your Life Story Personal Benefits For You The Writer

Life Story writing has the potential to provide a wealth of benefits and personal satisfaction for the *writer. I know this from other writing experiences* I've had along the way, in addition to writing my own story.

I have done journaling most of my life, and frequently scribble out thoughts as I work through personal issues of all sorts. Through writing, I frequently see experiences, conflicts and issues from a new perspective.

Sorting and clarifying

As I wrote my Life Story, I was able to *sort* and *clarify* old issues that originally seemed insurmountable, but what now appear to be the very foundation of my sound values.

So, contrary to re-experiencing painful feelings, I sensed feelings of joy, clarity and emotional release as I walked through these old memories. And many times I even had a good laugh, because now as an adult I could see the humor in many situations that wasn't apparent to me at the time.

Reframing

Writing our Life Story provides the opportunity for us to take a new look at old experiences and *reframe* them to our advantage. For example, I have spent a fair amount of time in my life focusing on the embarrassment of how I froze up, failed and was booed in front of a Big Ten College speech class.

I was so unable to handle this type of ridicule at that time in my life, that I seriously considered dropping out of college as a result of the incident. And while I didn't drop out, the incident did haunt me for years, but now seems like a laughable speck-of-dust in view of the speaking and writing accomplishments during my life.

I was able to reframe that five minutes of embarrassment that one time tore me down, into one of the most insightful lessons I have ever learned, one that launched me on a mission to overcome fear of public speaking and low self-esteem. The lesson I learned? Turn things around by using a negative to generate a positive! "This is my story. That's who I was, but this is who I am today."

Writing the Story Of Your Life gives you the chance to sort of package your life in a way that others can walk with you on what has been your journey from the past to the present, seeing your life unfold as you saw it.

Writing your story and sharing it with others gives you a great feeling of accomplishment and fulfillment, a sort of fresh perspective as you look over your life and experience the feeling of a job well done, "Here's my story, this has been my journey, and this is who and where I am today!"

Finding Fulfillment
Fulfillment comes from doing something worthwhile that we enjoy, doing it well, and making a contribution that will enrich the lives of others. People find joy, satisfaction and fulfillment in a variety of undertakings. Some knit, some play music, some hunt, some golf, some write, and some do it all!

I've found life writing to be much like an interesting life-enrichment project. As a result, I feel like I have lived two great lives. First, the actual life I lived and now the great life I re-lived while writing my life story!

So, Why Write Your Story?

Because it will be something very special for your loved ones while providing many personal benefits for you, the writer.

What personal reason(s) come to mind for you to write your life story, that will light your fire and provide the motivational fuel to complete the task?

What reasons for writing your story might motivate you to accomplish your goal?

_____

_____

_____

_____

_____

_____

_____

_____

_____

_____

4 - Getting Started Right
Unleashing
Your Greatest Potential

Our life story writing goals can be best achieved if we experiment to find,

- our best times,
- our best places, and
- our best methods to write.

When is the best time of day or night for you to work on your Story? Only you can answer that question. And, the answer is found by experimenting.

MY STORY - An Example

I write best when my other responsibilities for the day are taken care of. This does not always mean completing my other chores. Sometimes it means just getting them on a *to do* list so I can get them off my mind for now. By getting them on my list, I still get them done in a timely fashion.

I have a greater flow of ideas early in the day, during exercising, so I keep a note pad handy near my treadmill. However, I find that planned procedures and ideas sometimes go down the drain, so I don't depend on them completely. For example, I occasionally awaken at 3:00 a.m. with a great idea, and bounce out of bed to write before I lose the thought. Whenever my subconscious kicks in I don't want to miss the great story or idea it's prompting me to write. Works for me!

When Is Your Best Time of day/week To work on your life story?

Early morning, when it is quiet around the house, when you feel refreshed, and before anyone else is awake?

Before or after you get your routine work and responsibilities taken care of for the day?

In the evening, when you can finally relax and block off some time for yourself?

Just when is the best time for you to access your memories, reflect on events and experiences in your life?

Just when do you feel the most relaxed, open and receptive to experiences bubbling up that you would like to write about?

_____

_____

_____

_____

_____

_____

Where Is Your Best Place to Write?

In a room by yourself where it is totally quiet?

In a room or office, where others are working on their own projects all around you, but with minimal interaction with you?

In a noisy, bustling atmosphere, with many people around, involved in their own activities, but who are not interacting with you?

MY STORY - *An Example*
I write most effectively in places where there is a lot of activity and conversation going on around, but unrelated to me. Yes, I write most effectively at coffee shops and places like McDonalds.

Once I discovered this, I wrote the bulk of my 212 page life story, longhand, day after day, sitting in a booth at McDonalds. When I try to write at home, I find too many unrelated things to do before I get to writing.

Since I am left-brain-oriented, I can easily sit down at my home desk and organize papers, pay the bills and set up files. And if I don't pay attention to the know-thyself idea, I find that I have soon used up my highest energy and most productive time doing mundane tasks.

Solution? Get out of my home office and go to a coffee shop away from the routine, where I can really focus on getting words on paper.

There is a *best time and place* for you too, that fits your schedule, habits and personality.

Take time to find this best place, because it can make the difference between joy and drudgery in writing your Life Story.

_____

_____

_____

_____

_____

What Is Your Best Writing Method?

Life story writing can be accomplished using a variety of single methods or a combination of methods.

What method of writing might you find the most enjoyable while being the most productive?

- Using a word processing program?
- Talking stories into a recorder to write later?
- Talking stories into a recorder, to have someone else write later?
- Handwriting, using paper and pen/pencil?
- Using the latest electronic technology, phones? iPads? Computer?
- Using any combination of the above?

MY STORY - *An Example*

When I started to write my Life Story, I often sat down in front of my beautiful, wide-screen computer, but discovered that two or so hours later I had accomplished only one or two small paragraphs!

The problem for me at the computer trying to write my story? The teacher-in-me caused me to continually edit, re-write and play with the technology instead of *writing* fast and furious, using the focused writing technique, allowing thoughts and ideas to flow naturally.

The computer-method made it too easy for me to slip into my left-brain style and focus on the mechanics of writing rather than on capturing the story.

Of course, as explained in the Editing Blocker, (page 27), trying to edit and re-write during the initial writing of our stories is completely opposite of the method supported in this handbook. Yet, if we are not on guard, it is so easy to slip back into old, unproductive habits.

So what is the most effective method for me to get my stories down on paper? I soon discovered that I am most effective using

- *An old-fashioned paper and pencil* to scratch out little stories in first draft writing,
- The *Focused-writing* technique, *pretending while writing,* that I am *telling* my story to a friendly non-judgmental listener sitting across from me. (pages 15 - 18)

49

What method of writing allows *you* to be most productive? Be sure to explore all the possibilities, and choose a method that doesn't cause you to block the natural flow of subconscious memories as you write.

When choosing your best method, keep in mind that *in our first writing, it is the story* that is all important, not the wording, spelling, punctuation or grammar.

Our goal in the initial writing is to get the *story* down as it was experienced. We can go back later to rearrange details, make corrections in wording, spelling, punctuation and grammar.

Choosing the best method for you will not only make writing easier and more enjoyable, but will also result in getting the best stories down on paper.

Best advice? Know Thyself!

You might be surprised to discover what method or combination of methods will allow you to freely pump-out-the-words with no fear of writer's block.

Remember, *Getting Started Right With Your Life Story* is a key factor in both your success and enjoyment.

It might be helpful to review some of your other choices, to make sure you're on the most productive and enjoyable track.

Just what is *your* best story writing method?

Your Best Time Of Life To Begin Writing Your Story?

Life Story writing can be effectively s*tarted* any time in life up to the present. *Starting* means doing the groundwork, and *it's never too early to start that part of our writing project.*

During the early stages of our life there is much we can do on a daily basis to *prepare* for the writing part of the project that will come later.

MY Story - *An Example*
During the years that our children were growing up, I often made notes about some funny little thing they said or did, and often wrote out an entire little story to share at some family event.

Fortunately, I threw all of this *writing-stuff* in a file drawer with no thought of how valuable it might be for writing *my* Life Story. These miscellaneous notes and stories, combined with our detailed photo albums of family activities provided a wealth of priceless information, to be used years later when I finally wrote my story.

But in most cases, if we try to *write* our Life Story too early, we no doubt have a lot of unfinished business, a lot of living yet-to-do and not as much to write about.

However, there are exceptions. For example, A single young mother in her 30's might be in a situation that leads her to write a *memoir style* story focusing on a particular aspect of her life so far, that influences and changes the way she lives. Her title might be something like,

Me and Tony
Raising An Autistic Child
My Life So Far As A Single Parent

But in most cases, while we might not choose to *write* our story during our busy, education-child-rearing-career-years, we can be doing a lot during those years to make the task easier when we do decide to write.

Groundwork to make our writing easier later on, might include such things as,

- Recording important dates as they occur,

- *Making notes* about significant activities and events as they occur,

- *Writing little stories* about memorable experiences, when they are fresh in mind, to preserve memories that we know are too precious to lose.

- Journaling to maintain a chronological record of significant memories with the additional feature of describing feelings and interactions that surrounded the events.

When to write has to fit our life style, and is perhaps different for each of us. But it is noticeable that while many life stories are *started* during the *busy* years, most are finally *written after* many of life's main busy times,

- after our children have left the nest,
- after we have retired,
- when we seek enrichment, and
- when we have time to be more reflective about our life

If we wait too long to write our story, we risk the chance of having to deal with aging and health issues that make the project more challenging.

When is the best time to

GET STARTED
writing your Life Story?

Today!

When is the best time to
finalize your story?

You'll know when!

Make it a habit to keep writing your choice little stories, gathering them in a binder, according to the instructions in this Handbook. Then when *your* time comes to select and pull your little stories together into an organized Life Story, you'll have much of your work done.

Keep in mind, *Getting Started Right With Your Life Story* is a key factor for both your success and enjoyment.

Take a look at your stage of life. When do you think would be the best time of your life for you to *start writing* your life story? Why?

_____

_____

_____

_____

_____

What stories could you write now to store in your rough draft binder? Use extra paper if needed.

_____

_____

_____

_____

_____

_____

_____

5 - Choosing Writing Topics
Let Your Imagination Run Wild!

Remember, our job in writing about the past is to recall memories, not to create them. Our Life Story already exists. It has already been lived up to today. We merely have to recall the experiences so we can write about them. And prompts help us to recall those experiences.

Stories Waiting To Be Told
An easy way to get started with personal prompts is to make a list of topics that you already know you want to include in your life story. Most of us have a few zingers just waiting to be told.

For example, whatever the focus of my overall life story, I knew from the beginning that I wanted to include a little story about the *Ornery Rooster* on our farm. I also knew that I wanted to include the story about how we learned to drive in our old Model A Ford that had no brakes! And as one story-idea reminded me of another, my list began to grow.

Starter Sentences
Open ended starter sentences help us to kick-start the process of recalling memories. The list of starter sentences below is by no means complete. It is important to turn it into *your very own personal starter sentence list,* by continuing to add your own ideas.

Sample Starter Sentences

I want to tell about the time that

One of my fondest memories of childhood was

I'll never forget the time that

Life was really different when I was a kid, because

The achievement I am most proud of is (explain))

The funniest thing that ever happened to me was

The best years of my life were when

One of the biggest challenges during my life was

One of the biggest problems I had to overcome was

One thing that I learned the hard way was

Some things I would really like others to know are

One way I am proud to say I gave my best was

One thing I'll never do again

The hardest thing I ever had to do was

The happiest moment of my life was

The easiest thing I ever had to do was

The sadist experience I ever had was

What I learned from the __?__ experience was

If I had it to do over, I would

One thing I'll never forget is

One thing I did that I still regret is

One thing that was always hard (or easy) for me was

One thing I always loved to do was

The Memory Joggers List

A list of major events, such as *births, graduations, engagements, weddings, reunions deaths, losses retirements, achievements, etc. with* times and places, helps us to recall stories we would like to include in our overall life story.

Memory Jogger Ideas

MAJOR EVENTS
School years
marriage
college years
birth of children
military service
job-work-career
9/11
wars

FIRSTS
first home
first car
business venture
first cruise
first job
first child
first promotion
first date

THE EXTREMES
The Worst
The Hardest
The Easiest
The Most or Least
The Funniest
The Scariest
The Coldest
The Hottest

FAMILY ACTIVITIES
camping
boating
picnics
games
vacations
weddings
dining
celebrations

FAVORITES
favorite place to live
favorite job
favorite vacation
favorite place to vacation
favorite meal
favorite aunt, uncle
favorite season
favorite car
recreational activity
favorite entertainment
favorite holiday
favorite sport
favorite time of life

HOBBIES & INTERESTS
music
dancing
hunting
fishing
water skiing
 sports
singing
gardening
painting
celebrations
sewing
knitting
writing

OTHER
jobs
careers
places lived
travels
military service
children
awards
achievements
lessons learned
challenges

reading
swimming
motorcycling

REFERENCES
School Yearbooks
Report Cards
Photo albums
Newspapers
News clippings
Obituary records

Memories triggered by our senses

As we become more focused on writing, we begin to pay more attention to our senses. Have you ever noticed how your senses remind you of something past?

The bottom line for getting our mind to deliver old experiences worthy of our writing, is to increase our awareness to get the process started. Once started, one memory triggers another, and the process gains its own momentum.

Our senses of *sight, smell, taste, hear and touch* can trigger memories too. Consider the following potential story ideas triggered by one or more of our senses:

Example

Each time that I pick up a fresh loaf of homemade bread and a jar of homemade jam from the Farmer's Market, I get a warm feeling about the treasures we enjoyed during our great growing-up years. (the writer could go on to develop a story about the treasures enjoyed during early years on the farm that came to mind during a visit to the Farmer's Market).

Pay attention to your senses - turn your imagination loose, and see what story ideas might surface!

The Six Magic Words
What, When, Where, Why, How and Who
Let your imagination go wild, using these six words, to come up with or expand great story topics.

MY STORY - An *example*
From the Memory Jogger list, I chose *Our First Home.* Then I stirred my memory by thinking of questions using the *six magic words.*

What home?
What was it like?
How much did it cost?
What was the neighborhood like?
When did we buy it?
Why did we buy this particular home?
Where was it located?
How could we afford it?
How did we make the money for a down payment?
Who lived in the neighborhood?
Why did we like the home?

Then I wrote a little story, using some of these questions to help me make the story complete.

Here's just a small part of the story I came up with to demonstrate the idea.

The Sample Story Created
Our first home was a little ranch located on about two acres. We bought it in the fall of 1961 for $9500. It was located about two miles out of town. Our son was two years old and needed a little space to play. We had all been cooped up in a tiny apartment for too long!

Our new home had space for a garden, a sand box, swings, a place to pitch a tent and outdoor clothes lines to dry our fresh laundry. We even had space to get a new puppy.

We scraped up enough for a down payment on the home by taking extra music jobs. At first, we wondered if we would ever be able to keep up with the monthly payments with income from my first year teaching job, but we managed.

My story goes on, but do you get the idea of how to use one or more of the *six magic words* as writing prompts to develop a story.

The preceding ideas are sure to provide enough topics for getting started with our first few *little* stories. But keeping possible topics on hand to write about is an ongoing task. We have to continue to build and *maintain our own lists as ideas come to mind.*

Maintaining our topic lists requires us to team up with our brain, always on the alert for new ideas.

Our brain works in our favor as we become focused on writing our Life Story. As we write, we notice that one idea leads to another, one story leads to another and our project continues to grow.

We begin to pay more attention to the kinds of stories that we hear when socializing with friends. We let our mind wander a bit. Do any of these stories, including the ones *we* tell, bring back memories? If so, we make a note of the memory and add that to our topic list.

Don't waste time deciding whether or not to add a topic that you're not 100% sure of to one of your lists. Instead, just add it. You can always delete it later if it turns out that it doesn't fit.

Carry a note pad, or record a note on your cell phone. Most cell phones have a recording feature for leaving a quick reminder, until a more convenient time to add the idea to your list.

Our biggest challenge in the beginning? Getting the process started! Once we get the ball rolling, we'll have more topics to include in our life story than we need!

Keep adding any ideas that pop into your mind, from your socializing, reading, watching TV and other activities of daily living.

Maintaining the list is an *ongoing process*, so you will always have plenty of writing topics to choose from.

Use the space below to begin your own topic list. Use extra paper to add to the list as you get ideas

_____

_____

_____

_____

_____

_____

_____

_____

_____

_____

_____

_____

_____

6 - Choosing Your Style
The Common Life Story?
The Autobiography? Or The Memoir?

A Common (Fashionable) Life Story is about YOU, the main character, revealed to us through the stories and reflections you share in interesting, fascinating and entertaining ways.

Your story is really made up of a collection of smaller stories about you and your experiences, linked and blended together in some sort of logical sequence under an easy to follow theme.

Best of all, you don't have to *create* the story of your life. It has already been created, day by day, as you lived it. Your journey already exists in your memories. You only have to capture those memories that you would like to share, and get them down on paper.

You begin by writing these smaller stories step by step, one-story-at-a-time, without concern about where they might fit in your overall life story. Fitting them in comes later.

You'll tell us about your memorable, happy and good times, your successes and achievements. And, you might also tell us about some of your conflicts, challenges, failures and losses.

You'll let us see who you really are, as revealed through many stories about your life experiences and how you dealt with them.

You might include factual information like birth dates, wedding dates, etc., pertinent to the stories you tell. And while your stories might reflect *your* interpretation or spin, they should be *based on fact.*

When we finish reading your story, we'll have a much better understanding of the real you, from the inside out!

- We'll know more about what is important to you.

- We'll know what life has been like for you.

- We'll feel closcr to you as we relate to your life experiences, in both the good times and the challenges, from your perspective.

- We'll learn what really 'makes you tick' from the selected highlights of your life that you share, as well as from your interpretation of those memories.

- We might even get a peek at what is still on your bucket list, your dreams yet to fulfill.

- Your primary audience would be immediate family, relatives and acquaintances.

With the help of the information provided here, you'll gather all these bits and pieces, sort them out, wrap them in some kind of theme under a unique title, that brands you as the main character, star and author of your cherished Life Story.

This common style life story has become more popular and fashionable, as more and more people are writing stories about their life.

You might want to check out two other styles often used to describe the life writing process, the autobiography and memoir styles. Each has a slightly different approach.

The Autobiography is a life story that someone writes about him/her self, covering the writer's entire life span, usually chronologically, from birth to present. A *Biography* contains similar content, focus and style as an *Autobiography,* except the *Biography* is written by an author, not by the person who lived the life. The one term *Autobiography* will be used herein to describe the contents and theme common to both the autobiography and the biography.

The *Autobiography* is usually a bit more formal than the more casual, *Common Life Story*, and includes a wealth of factual and statistical information. There is usually more emphasis on the "what's", "where's" and "when's" vs. an interpretation of selected life experiences by the writer.

After reading your autobiography, we might know a lot about where you lived, traveled and worked, but we might not know a lot about *the inner YOU*. We might know what you did, but might not know much about your feelings, your dreams or how you faced problems in your life.

This approach to life writing is often used by people who are/were highly visible to the greater population, such as presidents, other leaders and entertainers like Elvis. However, this approach is a matter of choice and is available to all.

Many examples of this style are available on the internet and in local libraries for you to examine.

The Memoir Style is a more focused approach, where the author writes about a particular aspect of life and how it influenced various other parts of his/her life.

For example, a person might write a memoir about growing up in a family where alcoholism and domestic violence were rampant, and focus on how this affected the writer's entire life, positively and negatively.

The contents of this life story would then be chosen to support this focus. An example of a title might be, *How I Lived A Life In Hell, The Bottle And Domestic Violence.*

A story written with this tighter focus would no doubt appeal to an audience beyond the writer's family, interested in or affected by this specific issue.

It might also be of interest to readers interested in stories with conflict, conflict resolution, family issues or family relationships. In this respect, a genuine Memoir is perhaps a more marketable and profitable project, if your goal is to write and publish to a broader audience beyond your family.

Based on my experience - the style decision is best made after we have written several smaller stories. Writing seems to take on a momentum of its own and a natural theme and style begins to surface.

Therefore, it might be helpful to review this chapter later before making a final decision on style.

Based on what you know about the three types of life stories, which type would you like to write, and why?

_____

_____

_____

_____

_____

Who would be your main audience for the style you are considering?

_____

_____

_____

_____

Clarify how you think the style you are considering might appeal to the audience you have in mind?

_____

_____

_____

_____

_____

IF you decide on a *Memoir Style*, what would your overall message or theme be?

_____

_____

_____

_____

_____

_____

_____

_____

_____

7 - Goals and Decisions
A Long Range Look

Deciding on Life Story writing goals and making some early decisions can save you time, energy, money, and hours of frustration. *Following are some things to consider before using the options checklist.*

What Are Your Writing Goals?

How far do you want to go? The possibilities for your writing efforts range from writing a few little stories and storing them in a loose leaf binder, to writing a complete story of your life and presenting it in a bound hard-cover book.

But keep in mind, if you go no further than writing a few stories and placing them in a loose leaf binder, your efforts are worthy to pass on to your family.

Maybe you'll choose to write a few stories, then take a break, and return to add stories at your leisure. The choice is yours.

The Goal Options Chart will help you to decide how far you want to go.

Preserving Your Story - Your Choice.
What is your favorite media for preserving your story? Years ago, there was one anticipated end result for life writing, and that was to publish a hard cover book.

Nowadays, the media options for preserving your life story are almost endless, with the explosion of modern technology.

When we choose some form of electronic media for preserving our story, the question often arises concerning whether or not it is necessary to *"write"* the story.

YES! writing is necessary for many reasons, whatever the latest technology you might choose to record your story.

Finally, if you decide to take your story to a printer, you'll save yourself a bundle of time, energy and money if you know ahead of time what questions to ask.

Unclear goals and unanswered questions can make any project seem overwhelming and frustrating. Therefore, the purpose of providing information here is to help you avoid these feelings, and make your life story writing experience easier, more fun and enjoyable.

Perhaps you're not ready to make decisions about how far you want to go with your life writing project, or how you would like to preserve your writing.

But, *knowing the options ahead of time* and where to find the information when you're ready should provide a sense of relief that will allow you to concentrate on continuing to write your stories step by step for now.

Goal Options

Life Story writing has many options for your final product, concerning,

- How far you want to go with your writing, ranging from writing just a few stories to writing a complete bound book,

- How much and what kind of support material you want to include in your final product,

- How you want your completed story packaged if you choose to print it, ranging from loose-leaf binding to bound book binding,

- What modern media you want to use to preserve your life story if you decide not to print and bind it in some form.

- Who will do the writing - you or your hired biographer?

- Perhaps the biggest option is how far you want to go with your project. While it may be too early for you to set a writing goal, there are some important things you should know:

Whether you end up with only a few little stories preserved in a loose-leaf binder or with a complete life story presented in a bound hard-cover book, your efforts will no doubt be cherished as a Precious Gift by your family.

A bound, hard cover book of your story might be the ultimate goal. *But it is not the only acceptable goal. Any goal between a few stories and a complete bound book is acceptable and worthy of achieving. Don't let the bound-book syndrome stop you before you get started!*

You might choose a lesser goal to get started, and then change it to a higher goal when you get bitten by the life story bug!

You can write your story at your own pace, in a few weeks or over a period of years. Therefore you may actively write for awhile, take a break and return for more writing at your leisure. The most important thing is to *get started.*

Play around with the lists of options below for content, support, binding and media, until you come up with a goal that is realistic and achievable for you.

Keep in mind, you have the option to change your goals by cutting back or expanding as you work through the writing process.

Well chosen goals will not only motivate and inspire you, but will also result in your project being fun and enjoyable!

Ways To Preserve Your Story

Life Story writing takes a lot of thought and effort, b*ut, the results are priceless!* So, it is extremely important that we

choose a way of preserving our results that is

- a workable process for us now, and

- provides a realistic way to share our story for years to come.

There are many ways of preserving your story, ranging from the very traditional handwritten story to the very up-to-date electronic methods.

Here is a brief description of some of the common ways.

Traditional Writing
This style consists of handwritten stories stored in some form of loose leaf binder. The loose leaf style provides the advantage of adding, removing and rearranging pages and stories as you progress.

Word Processing
As of this writing, Word Processing is probably the most popular, fastest, easiest and efficient way of getting words on paper. It provides the flexibility of being able to easily rearrange whole blocks of content, make corrections with ease, and finally, to print any or all pages at the click of a mouse.

Word processing software also provides the opportunity for you to save written material on your computer or on some type of portable storage device, like a CD or flash drive.

This is a handy feature for transferring your story to others for reading on their computers. It is also a handy feature for delivering your story to a printing service, if you decide to have it printed commercially.

Audio Recording
Many people decide to capture their stories on some sort of recording device. These might consist of a small hand-held recorder or a larger desktop recorder.

Another option is the recording feature found on most computers nowadays that allows you to talk into the microphone while the computer records your story. You can then print your story or transfer it to a printing service on a storage device.

Or, you might choose to have your story recorded by a commercial recording company. But if you choose this approach, it is very important to have a written copy of your story to work from. (See pp. 31 and 78)

Life Story Video
A video of you sharing your story is another popular method that can be done with either a home video camera or by a commercial recording service. As with audio recording, a written copy of your story is important to work from. (See pp. 31 and 78)

Electronic Publishing

With the rapid changes in information technology, it is possible to send information around the world in seconds without leaving our home. Memos can even be quickly recorded on many of our cell phones, lest we forget them in our ever busy life style. And of course, we can prepare our stories so they may be read on some brand of electronic book, such as Kindle.

Life Story Writing Services

Nowadays, we can even submit factual information to publishers who specialize in preserving our life story online, based on the information we provide.

But keep in mind, having a hard copy of your writing is important, even though you may choose to distribute it to your family and friends through some form of electronic media. (See pp. 31 and 78)

The Goal Options Checklist

In your effort to decide how far you want to go with your life story writing, check those features in the lists on the next two pages, that you would like to have as a part of your *initial* project.

You can add or erase from the GOAL OPTIONS CHECKLIST as you progress through your writing experience.

Use the extra spaces to list additional goal options.

GOAL OPTIONS CHECKLIST
Page 1

	Desired Content
	Miscellaneous collection of several stories
	Sequenced collection of stories
	Stories edited, refined, enhanced
	Content organized into chapters
	Completely finished, printer-ready life story
	Desired Front Support Features
	Title Page
	Copyright Page
	Table Of Contents
	Introduction
	Acknowledgements
	Dedication
	Writer's Intent
	Brief Personal Statement
	Desired End Support Features
	Special Photos
	Significant Events Chart
	Certificates - Awards
	Recognition and Achievements

GOAL OPTIONS CHECKLIST
Page 2

	Bindings
	Loose-leaf binder
	Three-prong style folder
	Inexpensive glued binding
	Spiral binding
	Standard soft cover binding
	Standard hardcover binding
	Printing - Media Options
	Single hand-written copy
	Word-processed copies
	Printer-ready word-processed master
	Saved on a CD or flash drive
	Home audio recording
	Commercial audio recording
	Home video recording
	Commercial video recording
	Saved online by commercial online services

Do I Need To "Write" My Story?

Yes! Let's ask those who recorded their stories on the old 78, 33, or 45 records, the 8-track tapes or cassette tapes.

It's my guess that these writers don't currently have much of a way of passing their legacy *unless* they also preserved their stories in writing, or kept re-recording as technology changed.

If they preserved their stories in writing (hard copy), they might still be sharing them, in the written form or perhaps even through the use of the latest electronic technology.

Keep in mind the importance to you and your family of capturing your story and putting it in some sort of format that can be shared by those important to you.

But, whatever method you choose for your *final product*, traditional writing, word processing, audio recording, some type of modern media or having someone else preserve your story,

The bottom line is, *your story writing will be best and safest if you first prepare a hard copy - either a printed word processed copy or a handwritten copy.*

Why Is a hard copy important?
If you decide to audio record your Life Story, it will be more organized and captivating to your reader, if you either read it or speak from an organized and properly sequenced outline.

If you decide to use modern information technology to get your story out to your readers, you will either need to record into the electronic device or somehow get hard copy into the device.

If you decide to use a Life Writing Service, you will need to provide information in some form, otherwise how will they know what to write about?

Whatever method you choose to preserve your Story, whatever your final product might be, *an original hard copy that you can file in a safe place is important for the safe preservation of your Life Writing for years to come.*

Modern technology comes and goes, but the written language is a stable, trustworthy old method for safe preservation of stories.

-- See Chapter 2 --
WRITER'S BLOCK #5, THE WRITING IS
UNNECESSARY BLOCKER

Questions To Ask Your Printer
Life Story planning can save you time, energy and money, especially when it comes to preparing your final product. This is especially true If your final format will call for printing.

By knowing what format your printer will require before you finalize any of your drafts you will be able to write your stories in that required format as you go. This is better than being surprised by your printer's requirements and having to convert or re-do all your writing to meet those requirements.

Also, you will be able to make cost decisions before you get too far into your project. Decisions about the following features can have a significant effect on the overall cost of your project.

- color vs. black and white,
- type and weight of paper and
- style of bindings

Following are some questions you might ask your printer concerning submission of your final project, before you get too far along with your writing.

How will your printer want you to present your manuscript?
- Word processing? (name and release?)
- Electronically? (software name and release?)
- Hard copy (printed manuscript)?
- Saved on a CD?
- What other requirements will your printer have?

Layout, File and Font Details
- Page layout?
- Margins?
- File types
- Font size

Bindings
- What kind of bindings will your printer offer?
- What are the advantages, disadvantages of each?
- What are the costs of various types of bindings?

Black and White or Color
- Will your printer offer both color and black and white?
- Cost comparisons of color and black/white?
- Will your printer be able to reduce costs by offering color along with some black and white?

Total Cost - Deposit - Final Payment
- How much will your printer want for a cash deposit?
- What will the total cost be?
- When will the final payment be due?

Proof Copy and Completion Date
- Sample (proof) copy to approve before printing?
- When will the printing be completed and ready for you to pick up?

When you are ready to visit your printer, take along one of your final drafts to find answers to these and other questions before you get too far along with your work.

Not only will your printer be able to provide you with requirements and price information for the above, but he/she will also be able to help you make decisions as well as give you ideas by showing you samples of products finished for other customers.

Minimum Basic Features Desired
Make a list of the basic features of your finished product that you are sure you want your printer to know. Use extra paper if needed.

_____

_____

_____

_____

_____

_____

_____

_____

_____

_____

_____

8 - Polishing, Arranging, Shaping Your Stories To Fit

Life story writing involves writing many little stories that are later polished and seamlessly sequenced together to result in an overall story of your life.

Until now, you have spent your time writing these little stories, not knowing exactly how these little pieces might become a part of your big story.

From here on, in the step-by-step process, you will begin bringing these little stories together, using techniques to connect them seamlessly, as you build the overall story of your life. So be patient with yourself and keep writing!

If you have followed the step-by-step process so far, you have now arrived at a very exciting spot in your writing project.

By now, you have probably written several little stories and stuffed them in a loose leaf binder.

Hopefully, you have focused on *w-r-i-t-i-n-g* (not editing) so far, not giving much thought to how all these little stories might fit in to the overall story of your life.

And you need to continue writing little stories, even though we are beginning to look at the tasks of polishing, arranging and shaping your stories to fit into some sort of theme for an overall story.

Now, something new is about to happen. As you continue to write, you will eventually begin to see a theme emerge that will provide a way to organize your stories in some sort of natural sequence resulting in the overall story of your life.

Once this theme begins to emerge, you'll be ready to refine the little stories you've written, and fit them in the best places to support your overall theme.

As you refine, shape and re-write your stories to fit, you'll begin to see how you might add life to your writing by adding bits of dialog here and there.

And then comes the editing task – which might or might not fall within your interest or skill level. However, we quickly remember that, Editing is a separate task from our all-important story writing. And, unlike story writing, editing is a task that can be delegated.

Finally, as you begin to see your whole life story come together, you'll be so excited about your accomplishments that you'll be ready to make your stories even more authentic and interesting by adding photos from your own collection.

And who knows – you may even decide to add some interesting clip art or other graphics for the finishing touches.

Each of the tasks described above is explained in detail in other pages in this chapter. Take time to check out each topic carefully, as you begin to put the pieces together to *build the story of your life!*

Sequencing Stories
To Build Your Life Story

An overall life story is really

- a series of little stories,
- seamlessly connected one to another,
- in some chosen order
- to create or support an overall theme or focus.

After we have written many of the stories that we want to include in our overall life story, we must decide on a way to organize or sequence them so there is a *natural flow* of life experiences, from one to another, throughout.

We begin to think, "Oh, I now see that this story fits best over there, and another story would work best under this section." Get the idea?

Organization of your material into some sort of sequential pattern, with a brief transition from one story to the next will be easier after you have written several stories.

In fact, if you wait to organize until after you have written several stories, you will no doubt begin to see a *natural* theme or pattern emerging.

And since you are keeping your stories in a loose-leaf binder, you can move them around as you choose, until you find the best fit for each, to tell your Life Story as you want it told.

When you discover the best organization, the floodgates will open and you'll think of many more things to write about that seem to fit in your new-found structure.

Does the story of your life seem to naturally unfold around some sort of chronological sequence, telling about highlights between birth and the present?

MY STORY - *Example #1*
A Chronological Sequence

I organized my Life Story around the various places where I grew up and lived during my life, along with stories and experiences I wanted to include about life during each of these stages.

Here's a partial list of how I sequenced stories and experiences in My Life Story:

- Early Life on the farm
- Life/school in our 2nd home after selling the farm
- Life and living on campus - the college years
- Life and marriage - our very own first home
- Life, marriage and children - our first country home

Example #2 - Major Events Sequence

One of my friends wrote the story of his life, which he organized in a chronological sequence. However the bulk of his writing focused on his career in the military which he arranged in a sequence of the various stages and battles of World War II.

Example #3 - Problem/Resolution Sequence
Another friend who was adopted early in life wrote a Memoir describing his life-time experiences and feelings as an adopted child and how it affected his self-esteem.

His overall story was sequenced and organized around the theme beginning when he learned that he was an adopted child, stories of his life as an adopted child, the search for his real mother and finally, the discovery that his favorite aunt turned out to be his real mother.

Other ideas include organizing your story around various major events or stages in life, such as marriages, careers, family activities, various economic times, etc.

As you begin to organize your stories into your chosen sequence, you may begin to notice "holes" that need filling. This may call for another story or some sort of transition paragraph to smoothly move the reader on to the next story.

Here is a summary list of some common ways of sequencing stories:

In chronological order, by
- places lived, careers,
- major events in our life
- school, higher education, careers, retirement
- single, married, child rearing, empty nesting
- single life, parent, and then grandparent
- family, holidays, vacations, retreats, travels
- a mixture of any of the above

Brainstorm ways to organize and sequence your little stories to end up with one, beautiful, big story about you and your life, the way YOU want it told.

Take time to carefully check out each of the following Handbook topics, as you build the story of your life!

Refining And Shaping Your Stories

Writing our life story involves refining our little rough draft stories to fit into our 'big' story, seamlessly and naturally.

First, we decide *where* we would like the story to fit, Next, we *re-write* the story, shaping and slanting it (see details below) to support the context of where it is being used.

This re-writing may involve,

- Including more details than were in our original writing,

- Removing some of the details that were in our original writing,

- Changing the overall focus of the story to blend in with other material where it will be placed,

- Enhancing the story with dialog, photos and/or graphics, to make it more interesting, more meaningful and life-like.

MY STORY–An Example - Refining and Shaping.

In my Life Story I wrote about building a play house for our children. The main focus of the original story was on design and construction of the playhouse. But when I began organizing the stories to be used in my overall life story, I decided to include the playhouse story in a section about our home and the neighborhood during that particular time in my life.

However the story needed a little additional material to change its focus from the details of construction to a broader focus on what we considered an ideal neighborhood for raising our children.

So to make it fit I re-wrote the original story to include more than our experience of drawing up plans, getting lumber and other details of the building process.

The re-write included additional information about the neighborhood families and their children who used the playhouse along with our children, and went on to tell about the rich experiences all the children enjoyed on the two acres of land they played on in the neighborhood.

The re-written story added interest and quality, and transitioned nicely into the part of my life story telling about our life at that particular home, during that time of my life.

Another Example - #4 -Changing a story's focus.

In the small village where I live, there once was a vacant lot for sale, located at the edge of town, not far from the rail road tracks. It was also located on the river's edge near a bridge and across the street from an old-but-still-operating cider mill and cider-mill-store.

The lot was zoned for single family housing. However, potential buyers were turned away by the location near the rail road tracks, the bridge and the cider mill.

The lot remained on the market for several months with a significant loss of value, until one day an investor saw potential in the site from a different perspective.

He purchased the lot for a very low price, and then sold it later for a much higher price. He explained that realtors mistakenly showed the lot as if a home would be built *facing the bridge and cider mill, and be in view of the rail road tracks.*

But, the investor saw it from a different perspective.

Fast forward -

A beautiful home now stands on this site, with gorgeous windows, a majestic deck overlooking the ever rippling river, and is cushioned from surroundings with appropriate landscaping.

Only a quarter of a turn away from the distractions and toward the beauty of the river, nearly doubled both the monetary and aesthetic value of the lot!

Consider the variety of ways this story might be used by adding or subtracting a few details to change the focus, while still telling the true story.

A story focused on,

- The beauty of a river?
- The importance of the proper training of Realtors?
- How to make (or lose) money in real estate?
- The value of considering all perspectives

I have used this true story in a variety of speaking situations over the years to demonstrate to listeners the importance of at least considering a fresh, new perspective.

Bottom line?
A story might be used for a variety of purposes, and depending on where and how we decide to use it, we might expand, cut down, slant and/or change the focus of the story to support and fit in with surrounding content, while still telling the true story.

Take time to check out these other Handbook topics carefully, as you bring the pieces together to build the story of your life.

Editing Your Stories

Life story writing and editing are two completely different tasks. As life writers, our main job is to,

- Access our memories to come up with the stories we have lived, and then to
- Get the stories down on paper.

We write our stories non-stop, without editing as we write. We know that trying to edit while we write results in writer's block, and inhibits the process of recalling memories. Therefore, we learn to write first, and edit later.

The ideal time to edit is when we're deciding *if and where* a particular story we've written fits into our overall life story.

- First, we decide where the story fits in our overall story,

- Then we re-write it to fit seamlessly in the context of where it is being used,

- And finally, we edit it (or have it edited) to make corrections in grammar, punctuation and spelling along with any other changes needed to make our writing flow smoothly and accurately.

Editing involves "fixing" the *obvious* and the *not-so-obvious*. We might consider fixing the *obvious* ourselves, but if editing is not one of our strong skills, we might consider getting the help of a friend or professional more skilled in this area to find and fix the *not-so-obvious*.

Fixing The Obvious

You will no doubt be able to fix without help, many of the obvious grammar, punctuation and spelling errors that resulted from writing your stories quickly, just to get your *story* on paper.

If you use a computer, *spell check* will help with this task as will other built-in technologies that help us to locate and correct other kinds of grammatical and writing errors.

Fixing The Not-So-Obvious

Since you, the author, are *so close* to the content, it is very easy to gloss over errors that might be more easily visible to first time readers. Therefore, you might consider having different proofreaders for different purposes. For example, you might consider,

- One proof-reader to check for errors in grammar, spelling and punctuation,

- Another proof-reader to see if transitions from one story to another are understandable and flow seamlessly,

- Another to make sure stories are complete and understandable by checking to make sure that important pieces of information are not missing.

Sources of help for editing

One source of help you might consider is a high school or college student who has proven grammar and writing skills. Contact English Departments at local high schools and colleges to inquire about finding an excellent English student who might like to take on this task to make a little extra cash.

You might also find a teacher who is interested in editing your material, to earn a little extra cash.

College students specializing in teaching and or language often post editorial services as a way to earn extra income.

Finally, you might also find editorial help posted in your local library. Ask the librarian if he/she knows of any such postings or services.

And what if you don't find any immediate offers from the above sources? Then go to the sources mentioned above and post *your request for editorial services*, or run a brief ad in a local paper.

Certainly, you want to do your best with grammar, punctuation and spelling, but keep in mind, your main audience for your Life Story will be your children and family, and they will be absorbed reading your interesting stories, not checking to make sure every "i" is dotted or every "t" crossed!

Remember, Your Main Job Is Writing Your Life Story. You can get someone else to edit it!

Of course, if you intend to publish a book of your story through a major publishing company, for selling to a large market, the editing department of the publisher will offer assistance in taking care of editorial details for you.

If we all wait to write our Life Stories until we have *perfect* grammar and punctuation skills, there wouldn't be many Life Stories written in the world!

Take time to check out the following topics carefully, as you put the pieces together to *build the story of your life:*

Using Dialog To Bring Life To Stories
Our Life Story Writing moves to a higher level of interest and reality when we use bits of dialog in selected places.

What is dialog?
Dialog is a conversational exchange between two or more people, indicated in written stories by the use of quotation marks.

Why bother with dialog?
Occasional use of dialogue makes stories come alive and more interesting than stories presented entirely in narrative form.

MY STORY - An Example #5 - *without dialog*
First, read the following rough draft version of a story about our children's camping interests, before I re-wrote it using dialog.

Example #5
Camping – Our Favorite Sport!
The original version - without dialog*

Camping interests surfaced early for our three children (The Three-J's). They wanted to take advantage of our 2+ acres at our country home to pitch their tents down on the secluded, back part of our property.

Following is my original version of the story, before adding dialog. The little story demonstrates that a strong interest and persistent attitude are hard to hold back!

The Story without dialog:
Our bold little warriors ages 5, 7 and 12 decided to camp overnight on the back of our two-acre lot. I tried every reason I could think of, short of using fear, to talk them out of it.

But the more I talked, the more they sensed *my* fears, until finally, the truth humorously struck me, when they told me they were not afraid, and I responded that I was! *End of story without dialog.*

Now read the full and final version of the story that was re-written using a little dialog between me and my little campers, and included in my life story,

*The Ornery Rooster
And Other Humorous Encounters,
My Story So Far*

Example #6
The re-written version of the Camping Story
Camping – Our Favorite Sport!
dialog added

Our bold little warriors ages 5, 7 and 12 decided to camp overnight on the secluded back area of our two-acre lot. I tried every reason I could think of, short of using fear, to talk them out of it.

"You might get too cold," I said.

"We'll take blankets." **Joe** said.

"It might rain"

"We'll take raincoats." **Jamie** argued.

"Maybe you'll get hungry."

"We'll take a lunch." **Jen** persisted.

But the more I talked, the more they sensed *my* fears, until finally, the truth humorously struck me when one of them said,

"Don't worry Dad. We're not afraid."

And in a burst of laughter I could only respond,

"Yes, but I am!"

I'm sure you'll agree, from the above example, that adding even a little dialog here and there, in selected places, creates more interest and reality, and brings the story alive.

Basics for using
quotation marks in dialog

Periods and commas always go inside quotation marks.

- Question marks and exclamation points go inside quotation marks, *if* they are a part of the quotation. They go on the outside *if* they are *not* a part of the quotation.

- Each time the speaker changes in a conversation, the dialog should begin in a new paragraph.

The above basics will no doubt be sufficient for most of your use of quotes, however you can easily find an abundance of *free information* online to help with specific situations by searching terms like,

- punctuation,

- punctuation rules, or more specifically,

- how to use quotation marks.

Take time to check out the following and other topics carefully, as you Build Your Life Story.

Enhancing Your Stories
Using Photos, Graphics and Verses

Photos

Our Life Story is enhanced and made more authentic through the use of photos, placed appropriately throughout our writing. Photos bring life and reality to our writing.

A picture truly carries a message that might otherwise take hundreds of words to convey.

And of course, the best photos are those from our own collection that document our stories and our life first hand.

Following are some ideas and suggestions for using photos.

- Select photos to bring focus to the content on the page where you want to place them.

- Layout your pages with discretion, using balance as you place photos on a page, much as you would carefully place items when you decorate a room.

- Don't overdo your use of photos. Keep your main purpose in mind. You're writing a Life Story and the purpose of photos is to support and bring life to your stories.

- Check out the latest/best computerized photo software for home use as well as the self-service photo departments in various local retail stores. Many have computer work stations for your use in editing and saving photos on a CD, complete with software to help you transfer the photos into your stories.

- Do not make copies of copyrighted photos without written permission. For example, most photos that we purchase as we progress through the grades in school are copyrighted. Another example: photos taken by excursion or entertainment companies, such as cruise companies are often copyrighted.

- Use photos from your own camera. These make stories more authentic while avoiding the copyright issues.

Graphics - Clip Art

The use of clip art is another great way to enhance your stories with graphics. This art form provides a multitude of choices for captivating various emotions and other expressions that add clarity and meaning to your written copy.

Once you identify the exact message you want to get across to your readers, find the exact clip art piece to nail it down! And with your use of clip art, your readers will see that a 'drawing' is truly worth a thousand words!

C - A - U - T - I - O - N

While there are thousands of pieces of clip art to be found on the web and on clip art CD's that you can purchase, many are copyrighted and cannot be used without written permission and/or without paying royalty fees.

Don't overlook the possibility of you or someone in your family creating a few pieces of your own 'clip art.' For example, children are often very creative and able to produce a drawing to represent a message that will bring more attention than any purchased art work. Try it: Ask one of your children to draw a picture of your home - and then use it in an appropriate and related part of your story. You'll find that it will get much more attention than most photos!

Memorabilia
Adding various pieces of memorabilia is also a great way to enhance and give meaning to your stories.

Consider including appropriate copies of letters, notes, posters, and other materials that relate to your stories and brought meaning to your life.

These memorable pieces not only add variety and interest to your writing, but they also help to bring family and friends into your stories.

A Verse Of Self-Written Poetry
Poetry is a beautiful way to enhance and add quality to your Life Story, whether it is written by you or other family members.

Much like photos, an abundance of feelings, emotions, expressions and meanings can be expressed in just a few lines of poetry.

A lengthy, stand-alone poem that tells a story is fine if you are so inclined, but don't underestimate the effect of a simple, personally written verse slipped in appropriate places throughout your Life Story. A short poetic verse might also serve as a great caption for a photo.

However, if you use poetry other than something written by yourself, be sure to check for copyright and get permission before using it.

9 - Life Story Support Materials

Life story writing is strengthened by our use of appropriate support material. Certainly, the bulk of our writing which turns out to be the overall story of our life is the most important part of our efforts.

However, by adding appropriate support materials, we bring the finishing touches of meaning and clarity to our overall writing.

Support material falls into two categories, either

Front material
placed *before* our overall story,

or

End material,
placed *after* our overall story.

The order of writing and development, and the order of placement of the types of material in our writing usually follows this pattern:

First - We write our overall Life Story. This will be the bulk of our writing.

Next – We develop End Support Materials. We may begin to gather and develop END support materials as we continue to write our stories. These materials will eventually be placed after the last chapter of our overall life story.

Developing End Support Material - First

The main purpose of End Support Material is to help our readers put our life in perspective, relative to influential events, activities and relationships that transpired during our life time.

The various kinds of end support materials provide specific details on selected aspects of our life to help the reader better understand the effect of these surrounding influences. Though these details are not stories in themselves, they support the main story, adding meaning and clarity.

End Support Materials might include, but are not limited to:

- A Family tree
- Statements of Recognition for Various Achievements
- Certificates of Most Treasured Awards
- A Chronological Chart of Significant Events

 Check out the exhibited examples of *End Support Materials* from this author's own life story,

The Ornery Rooster
And Other Humorous Encounters
My Story So Far

Notice that *End Support Information* is presented here first in this Handbook, because it is best to prepare end support material before preparing front support material.

Preparing A Family Tree

Great Life Story Writing results from the inclusion of strong support materials to help our readers follow us as we piece together various parts of our lives.

A Family Tree, (a simple chart showing relationships between various family members) is one of the end support materials that has universal appeal in terms of adding meaning and quality to our life writing.

It is helpful to show the birth order of children in a family. And you may choose to be even more specific by showing birth dates.

As life story writers, it is important for us to realize that *our stories will be read by family members and others for years to come.* And, many of our readers will never have met the characters in our stories.

These readers need a family tree to help them understand the relationships within and between our families.

A *family tree* can be started as far back in family history as you choose. But starting with your grandparents or great-grandparents is sufficient for most life writers.

Of course, if genealogy is a main interest and focus of your writing, you'll want to go back far beyond your great grandparents.

A *family tree* is a must for the fashionably common style of life story writing.

MY STORY – An *Example*

As I wrote my story, I soon realized that if I needed the tree to help ME put my parent's families in perspective, our grandchildren, their children and other readers-to-come would certainly appreciate this piece of support material.

There were 13 children in my mother's family, and many died before I was born. I found it very interesting to gather and organize information about these aunts and uncles from both sides of my family, their birth order and who they married.

Other members of my family commented on the usefulness of the family tree, and often refer to it for clarification during family discussions.

Explanation Of Exhibit #1

Following is an example of a simple family tree created in my story, *The Ornery Rooster and Other Humorous Encounters. It shows,*

- the parents for both Minola and Floyd.

- the siblings for both Minola and Floyd, along with (spouse's names).

- where Minola and Floyd fit in their respective families by birth order,

- Minola and Floyd's children by birth order.

Exhibit #1 - Example - Family Tree - End Support

FRED BROWN Married RACHEL MOORE	Brown McInnis ↓	PETER McINNIS Married HELMA LINDSTROM
Children (spouse) Nora-died at birth Doris (Bohn) Bud (Doris) ↓	↓	Children (Spouses) ↓
MINOLA BROWN	← ***Married*** → ↓	***FLOYD McINNIS***
Bob Bob (Mazie) Edmund (Roby) Delbert (Sally) Dallas Fred (Lela) Evelyn (Ralph) Dick (Dorothy) Sonny (Vivian)	children ↓ Jean McInnis Pete McInnis ***Richard McInnis*** Ronald McInnis Doris McInnis	Donald (Delta) Salmaine (Sharkey) Vera (John) Laverne (Jack)

This table (exhibit #1) was made with Microsoft Word 7. From the **insert** menu, click **table,** then click **insert table** and follow the menu.

The possibilities are endless for Creating a simple family tree like this, or creating one that delves further back in family history for your story.

Some (artistic) writers prefer to sketch an actual tree, of various designs to show family relationships.

A very basic family-tree-design uses the tree trunk *to represent the parents, individual branches to represent each child, and balloon-style-name-holders* hanging from the branches for each grandchild.

Select a style that fits your needs - a computer-style chart like the one exhibited here or some other artistic design that gets the message across.

- OR -

Would you like to create a little interest and family involvement in your writing efforts ahead of time?

Have a contest between family members, inviting them to submit their idea of a family tree for inclusion in your finished product, with credit for their efforts!

Sketch Your Family Tree in the Worksheet below

Awards and Recognition

Most would agree, a life story is not complete without acknowledgement of some sort of *award or special recognition.*

Most of us have received some type of recognition sometime during our life that we are proud of however simple or basic it might be.

Recognition reaches us in a variety of ways, including,

- Formal Certificates of Most Treasured Awards
- Statements of recognition for various achievements
- Informal notes, greeting cards, home-made or hand-written certificates

As a parent, it has been my experience that some of the best recognition I ever received came from home-made cards and personally written little notes left on our refrigerator or on my desk.

Whether the recognition is for some major career accomplishment or as basic as Best Cookie-Baking-Grandma-of-the-year, it is worthy of including in the story of your life if it is meaningful to you.

MY STORY – *An Example*

Exhibit #2a is an example of a brief explanation of the Treasured-Awards I decided to display, to include along with the certificates, as end support information.

This is just a simple statement that shows how to introduce awards (or anything of value to you).

It gives you the opportunity to tell a brief story behind the award, such as how/why you earned it and why it is so important to you. This is placed with the award along with other end support materials.

You may choose to write about an award without showing a certificate - your choice.

Exhibit #2a
Below, is an example Of A brief Statement Explaining The Significance of An Award

I have been fortunate to receive a lot of both competitive and service awards over the years, but two awards, the Dean's Award that I received from Eastern Michigan University, College of Education, as Distinguished Lecturer of the year, and the Volunteer Of The Year Award that I received from The Michigan Hospice and Palliative Care Organization stand out in my mind as the most treasured.

(Only The College Of Education Certificate is displayed on the next page, as an example)

Exhibit #2b
Example of display
of basic award certificate

College of Education
Eastern Michigan University

2002

Dean's Award

Distinguished Lecturer
Richard McInnis

The 2002 <u>Distinguished Lecturer Award</u> is made to <u>Richard McInnis</u>. Mr. McInnis holds a bachelor's degree in business education and a master's degree in administration, both from the University of Michigan. He was a teacher at Dexter High School, an educational sales representative for a major publisher, self-employed in the real estate field, and a teacher in adult education centers.

For the past three years, he has supervised student teachers for EMU. He has provided outstanding leadership for other university supervisors of student teaching and his student evaluations have been extraordinarily high. Mr. McInnis' initiatives in improving our student teaching program have been both significant and well received by all those involved. He exemplifies to a high degree the attributes that we prize in all our full- and part-time Lecturers. We deeply appreciate his contributions to our programming.

Jerry Robbins, Dean

September 3, 2002

Preparing A
Significant Events Chart

Life Story writing takes time and energy, and you've worked hard to get this far. Now you're in the process of tying it all together by creating solid support materials.

There are no set types of end support materials that are required to put the finishing touches on your story. However the use of a Chart Of Significant Events seems to have universal appeal in terms of adding meaning and quality to life story writing.

MY STORY – *An Example*
The significant events chart that I included in my story, similar to the example of a partial chart below, is probably the most used and most liked of all support materials.

It is frequently used as a reference in family get-togethers and discussions when an important date or specific piece of information is in question.

It was developed by using Microsoft Word's *Page-Layout, Insert, and Table commands*. to create a 4 column table as follows:

A *year column*, beginning with the year of my birth,
An *age* column, a *grade/job* column and a significant event column.

You are encouraged to design your chart to reflect the sequence of factual information that clarifies and supports your story.

Begin your story at birth or wherever your life story begins and continue to your date of publication. In the actual chart that I used in my Life Story, I began recording information beginning with my date of birth and carried it through the date that I printed my Life Story.

I included information in the chart that was significant to me and supportive of my story, including dates of important changes in employment, anniversaries and birthdays of extended family members, dates of significant personal achievements and other information.

At-a-glance, the reader can see the most significant (most remembered) events in the writer's life for any year, from birth to the time my story was written.

The chart provides a chronological story of main events, and helps readers put our life in perspective.

Since the material for your chart can be gathered at any time during the writing process, it is *something good to work on when you're not feeling so creative in terms of writing stories.* In fact, gathering and organizing this material might trigger your memory for other stories to write.

Exhibit #3 - Example
Partial Chart Of Significant Events

YEAR	AGE	OTHER	SIGNIFICANT EVENT
1935			Birthdate March 7, 1935
1936	1		
1937	2		
1938	3		
1939	4		
1940	5	K	Started half days of school
1941	6	1st	Brother Ronald's Birth-Death. 8/41. 1st grade 9/41. Pearl Harbor 12/41. WWII began 12/41
1942	7	2nd	
1943	8	3rd	Sister Doris born 1/11/43
1944	9	4th	
1945	10	5th	1st atom bomb dropped 8/6/45. 2nd atom bomb dropped 8/9/45. Japan surrenders 9/2/45. Jean graduates from H.S.
1946	11	6th	Spring1946 we sold farm and moved to a home about two miles away on M-28.
1947	12	7th	Jean (sister) and Duane married 6/16/47
1948	13	8th	Pete (brother) and Gerry married 9/10/48
1949	14	9th	Salutatorian of McMillan 8th grade class. Seven students in the class. Started Newberry H.S. 9/49

A Partial Blank Significant Events Chart
For You To Experiment With

YEAR	AGE	OTHER	SIGNIFICANT EVENT

Developing Front Support Material - Last

After our story writing is completely done, we develop Front Support Materials. These will be placed in front of our overall Life Story.

We develop front support materials last because much of what we say in this section of our writing grows out of our experience in writing the main content of our overall story.

Front Support Materials include, but are not limited to information to,

- set the tone of your story,

- make your story easy to follow, and

- make your story interesting.

Examples From Author's Life Story
Check out the exhibited examples of Front *Support Materials,* in the next few pages of this Handbook, taken from this author's own life story,

The Ornery Rooster
And Other Humorous Encounters
My Story So Far

ACKNOWLEDGEMENTS

This is to acknowledge help from the following for their contributions to this writing project:

Joe, Jamie and Jen for telling me stories to write about that I had never heard,

Jean and Duane for help in clarifying details about the farm and for helping me with information about years and models of cars, and Cheri Braun for providing additional information and clarification on the Brown/McInnis family tree,

Shirley Atkins for providing a selection of pictures of Joe, Jamie and Jen, along with a variety of pictures of grandparents, relatives and vacation activities,

Jamie for her contribution of drawings in the camping and playhouse chapters, her work on the book cover as well as her encouragement to hurry up and write the book, and

Jeanie for getting up-to-date pictures of the old farm buildings, the M-28 house, the General Store, Columbus Township School and Newberry High School, her printing help and personal support while I became totally absorbed in the project.

Thanks To All!

INTRODUCTION

First You Must –
Read About The Ornery Rooster

Chapter 1, the story of The Ornery Rooster should
be read before any other chapters, to prepare you for
appearances of The Rooster in many other stories
throughout the book.

After reading about The Rooster in Chapter 1, you
might like to continue with the chapters in
numerical order, however you might choose to jump
around, picking and choosing stories according to
interest. The following information about how the
book is organized will help you in either case.

How The Book Is Organized
The book is divided into 24 chapters, sequencing
places lived and selected events in my life from birth
to the present.

Whatever Your Reading Style . . .
You might want to take a quick peek at the pages in
the back of the book before you start. The Brown-
McInnis Family Tree might be helpful if you need to
refresh your memory on names of relatives I use
throughout the book.

Guidelines For Including A Statement concerning the author's Intent

What overall feelings do you want your readers to take away from your life story?

For example, you might include a statement concerning the fact that while most lives have "ups" and "downs", your intent here is to focus on the positive, even though you may from time to time talk about some not-so-positive experiences.

Let them know what they can expect: A lot of laughs? A lot of surprises? Your story from *your* perspective?

MY INTENT - An Example From The Ornery Rooster Book

"I've tried to take a lighthearted look at the past so you'll find a lot of humor and enjoy a lot of laughs in these pages. However, like any person's life there are likely to be a few dark moments – but don't let that scare you away, because the overall focus of this book is on the positive."

Guidelines
For Preparing A Dedication Page

What is a Dedication?

Who do you feel most indebted to for accomplishing this project, or for life in general? The Dedication is different from The Acknowledgement. The Acknowledgement gives credit for help and support specific to this project.

The Dedication is more personal. It's a place to tell us who has really inspired you, not just during the writing of your story, but during your life in general.

Who lights your fire and keeps you going? This might be a family member, or perhaps a life mentor, or someone who has taught you valuable life lessons, or perhaps even your dedication to a cause.

The next page is an illustration of a simple dedication page from *my life story,*

The Ornery Rooster
And Other Humorous Encounters
My Story So Far

Exhibit #6
Example Of Dedication Page

My Story So Far

Dedicated

To

JOE, JAMIE, JEN

And

JEANIE

Exhibit #7 -Example Of The Layout Of A Table Of Contents to Include as front support information	

-- *REMINDER* --
(Wait to Prepare The Table Of Contents until LAST,
after all of the pages have all been numbered!)

TABLE OF CONTENTS

CHAPTERS

Exhibit #8
Example of Cover Design and Title

The Ornery Rooster

And Other Humorous Encounters

My Story So Far

by
Richard McInnis

Guidelines For
Cover Design And Title

Finally, your life story is complete, and you're ready to give it a title, a subtitle and cover design that will work together to give your reader an idea of what to expect inside.

And an easy way to get the title and cover design to work together, is to

- Decide on the Title and Subtitle first, and then
- Design the cover to support the Title and Subtitle

Following are some reflective questions to jog your memory and help you to come up with an interesting title.

To get started, feed your subconscious by making a few notes as you carefully consider each of the following questions,

- What is the overall focus of your book?
- What did you really write about in your book?
- How did you overcome hardships?
- How and why did you succeed?
- How, where and why did you fail?
- How would you describe your overall life so far? Easy? Difficult? Challenging? Fun? Sad? Satisfying? Wonderful? Exciting? Boring?
- Who will your readers be?
- What will they be looking for?

- What overall message do you want to leave
- How did you arrive at where you are today?
- What theme did your stories take on as you wrote?

Make a list of all the title ideas you come up with, and keep adding to the list as you get new ideas and make changes.

It may take a few days for you to come up with just the right title and subtitle. But don't be too hasty.

Trust that your subconscious is working and will pull all this information together to deliver a winning title for your Life Story.

Once you've decided on a title and subtitle, you're ready to design your cover.

Cover Design
Keep in mind, that the cover design should support (work together with) the title and subtitle.

Your cover should,

- Be pleasant to look at
- Tell a little story in itself
- Capture the reader's attention
- Set the scene for what's inside

Read my story beginning on the next page about how I arrived at my Life Story Title and cover design.

MY STORY – *An Example*

Here's how I arrived at the title, subtitle and cover design for my life story,

The Ornery Rooster
And Other Humorous Encounters,
My Story So Far

First, I wanted readers to get the idea right from the beginning that they would find a lot of humor in my book, because within our family they already knew me for my sense of humor and funny stories.

Next, I wanted everyone to know that this is only *my story so far*, and that I have a lot of living to do, so there might be more to come.

As I wrote about my life growing up on our farm, memories of our *Ornery Rooster*, who was a real part of my life, kept popping up.

Yes, I really did have to deal with this Ornery Cuss on a daily basis as I passed his chicken house on my tricycle-travels between the cow barn and our house.

As you might expect, I have many now-funny stories to tell about how I managed to survive, in the presence of this ornery beast on a farm that he thought belonged to him!

Finally, one day my subconscious delivered me the idea of using the Rooster as a metaphor to talk about life nuisances in a light hearted way. Bingo!

And my cover design for The Ornery Rooster Book?

- Near the top of the front cover, I used a color-sketch of the Ornery Rooster, prepared by my daughter.

- Next, I used a font for the title and subtitle that suggests humor and fun.

- I used color for the title and black for the subtitle.

- Next, I included my name in black using a small font.

- Finally, I used a photo from our own album, of the mile-long sandy road to our farm, that we walked every day, to and from our school bus.

And each time I look at my cover I *travel* that road again, and it takes me back to the memories of growing up on our farm.

And each time that we return to my old home town, I drive up that still sandy road to our old farm, and reminisce,

As I look off into the distance And think to myself,

This is me.

This is my Story.

Legal
Suggestions
You Should -or- Should Never

Legal advice is beyond the scope and purpose of this Handbook.

Therefore, specific information on copyright laws are not provided here, other than to say that,

- It is suggested that you do copyright your Life Story for your protection as sole owner of the material, and

- You should never use copyrighted material of others without written permission from the copyright owner,

- When in doubt, check it out!

  And finally,

- You should seek legal advice about specific Copyright and other legal questions. You will find information about copyright laws and procedures online, however you will probably still need legal advice to interpret and help you understand the laws.

Exhibit #9 -

Example of a copyright and title page
The Title of your book and the Copyright Notice should appear together on a separate page that contains **only** title and copyright information. The page should *be placed immediately after the front cover.*

The Ornery Rooster

And Other Humorous Encounters

My Story So Far

By

Richard McInnis

Copyright © July 23, 2009 by Richard McInnis
6930 Wellington Drive
Dexter, MI 48130

Protected by Copyright Law. All rights reserved. Reproduction of this book or any part thereof, by photocopy or any other means, is a violation of Copyright Law, and may not be made without permission of the copyright owner.

10 - Completing Your Project

Wow! You've written your life story. Your hard work (the writing) is done, and you are ready to package it to pass on to your cherished readers.

Now you are ready to add some finishing touches. Take your time with this part, to reflect on what you've accomplished. And above all, don't hesitate to bask in your achievement!

Re-Evaluating
Goals And Decisions

Now that you've finished your writing, your first task in completing your project involves going back to re-evaluate   goals and decisions you made earlier, concerning choice of binding, kinds of support material to be included and printing/media options.

Chances are, your writing has come out better than you expected and you might like to upgrade some of those decisions before making multiple copies.

Go back now, and
re-visit The Goal Options Chart

If your initial decision was to merely put together a sequenced loose-leaf collection of stories about your life, would you now like to upgrade that decision?

Now that you see how much you have accomplished you might like to bind your life story in a different way than you originally planned, such as with a spiral binding or a standard hardcover binding.

131

Ways To Preserve Your Life Story

Have you given any thought to including an audio recording of any parts, or of your entire story? How about a brief video where you talk about some particular event or time period of your life?

Now that you know more about front and end support materials, would you like to add more support information at the beginning or the end of your writing to help your readers?

One Last Look

Finally, once you have made these decisions and are ready to move ahead, it is time for a one final proofreading - one last browse-through, before making multiple copies.

YES, even though your stories have already been proof-read once, it is still important to personally give them *one-last-look* now that you have them in final form.

Saving Your Precious Hard Work

Before giving a printed copy of your story to someone else to proof read, be sure you have saved both digital and hard copies.

You have too much work involved in your project! Don't take a chance on losing it!

In fact, it is suggested that you have your writing saved in more than one place using various technologies. For example you might consider saving it in multiple places, such as on

- your main computer
- another computer
- A flash drive, or
- other storage device

Of course, technologies change rapidly, so you should consider saving your hard work on the latest and safest technology available at the time.

Preparing Multiple Copies

With all of your hard work done, you are finally ready to make multiple copies. Of course, how and where you decide to make multiple copies depends on decisions you made earlier in your writing process.

And finally, if you plan to take your life story to a printer to make multiple copies, you might want to

be sure you get the results you want
by re-visiting the topic,

Questions For Your Printer, pages 79-82

Important! - Get Proof Copies
Wherever you take your manuscript to get multiple copies made, ask for a single *proof copy* for your examination *before the final printing* of your order.

When you get the proof copy, check it page-for-page with a copy of your original manuscript, to make sure each page is as you expected and that nothing is missing.

Then, talk with the printer to make any adjustments needed before going ahead with multiple copies.

Whoopee!!
You're Ready To Celebrate!

It's time to prepare for the presentation of your wonderful gift to your cherished readers!

Presenting Your Gift

Writing your life story is hard work, but now it's payday! You deserve the joy of presenting your life story as a special gift to your cherished audience of readers, and this calls for a special event of your design, as formal or informal as you choose.

*Your
accomplishment
deserves the attention
equal to or above earning a high level degree,*

and

*don't you settle for less,
even if you have to throw the party
yourself!*

My Story – *An Example*

I chose a less formal occasion to present my written life story to family and children. Since camping has always been a main family activity that we love, I chose a summer camping trip planned as a family get-together with our adult children and grandchildren.

What a perfect opportunity to present my hard work in a relaxed setting, enjoying family activities around a camp fire, similar to those written about in my life story.

How would you like to present and celebrate your hard work?

Even though I presented my book at an informal family event, I still took the time to share a few words about my writing experience. Some ideas I used to guide me which might be helpful for developing *your* brief presentation are listed below.

Provide helpful information, but be brief, no more than 10 to 15 minutes, maximum. However, you might allow time for questions beyond the 10 -15 minutes. I included comments about,

- Why I decided to write a Life Story,
- My overall intent in writing my story.
- How my overall life story is organized.
- I made suggestions to help readers get the most out of my writing, explaining that the writing was arranged in a manner that allows them to conveniently jump around without losing meaning.

- I mentioned acknowledgements – those I wanted to recognize, thank and for what.
- I called attention to specific end-support materials, showing where they are located, how they are organized and how to use them.
- I included other brief comments appropriate for the experience and for the occasion.

However, I didn't talk about any of the stories or content of the book. I wanted to leave them in suspense so they would enjoy reading it!

And where do you find all the information you need to make your little presentation? In the front and end support materials of your story, that you've already developed! Not in the story section!

Be sure you keep your presentation brief. This is not the time to tell any stories you've written or to give away any punch lines.

Rather, it's time to whet appetites and make your listeners want to read your story.

It's also a time to enjoy your accomplishment. It will be perfectly normal to feel a burst of confidence and feeling of a job well done.

Congratulations!
You have prepared a precious gift that readers will cherish for years to come.

www.ingramcontent.com/pod-product-compliance
Lightning Source LLC
Chambersburg PA
CBHW070919290526
45795CB00001B/362